T0359818

**Other titles in the UWAP Poetry series
(established 2016)**

Case Notes

David Stavanger

David Stavanger is a poet, performer, cultural producer, editor and lapsed psychologist. His first full-length poetry collection, *The Special* (UQP, 2014), was awarded the Arts Queensland Thomas Shapcott Poetry Prize and the Wesley Michel Wright Poetry Prize. David co-directed Queensland Poetry Festival (2015–17) and is the co-editor of *Australian Poetry Journal* vol. 8, no. 2 – 'spoken', *Rabbit* no. 27 – Tense and *Solid Air: Australian and New Zealand Spoken Word* (UQP, 2019). David is sometimes known as Green Room–nominated spoken weird artist Ghostboy. These days he lives between the stage and the page.

David Stavanger
Case Notes

Poetry

First published in 2020 by
UWA Publishing
Crawley, Western Australia 6009
www.uwap.uwa.edu.au

UWAP is an imprint of UWA Publishing,
a division of The University of Western Australia.

Copyright © David Stavanger 2020
The moral right of the author has been asserted.
ISBN: 978-1-76080-119-9

 A catalogue record for this
book is available from the
National Library of Australia

Cover design by Becky Chilcott, Chil3
Typeset in Lyon Text by Lasertype
Illustrations by Eddy Burger
Printed by Lightning Source

 uwapublishing

Unlike human beings who either dupe others or are duped, dogs will give an honest bark at the truth.
Other dogs bite their enemies, I bite my friends to save them.

Diogenes

Contents

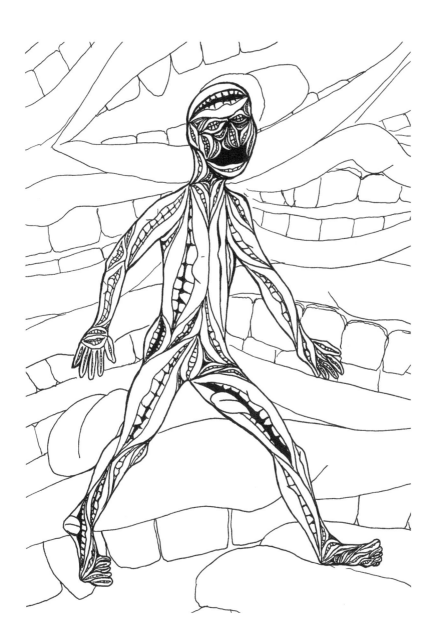

one must utilise every part of the animal [when faced with one's own fears]

I am hearing voices

banging pots [something living in my skin] trucks
picking up what's left of the week

a man appears at the front fence, wants
to know if the cattle dog is friendly

"I'm not sure but you're welcome to enter"

the man asks if he will be safe
on the other side of the bolted gate

looks first at our dog's bared teeth
then my worn underpants

he wants guarantees that can't be given

I say "you should be okay, just don't touch
his head or make sudden movements"

even though our dog's yellowed teeth
could no longer puncture
a meter man's shaking hand

I tell him it's a dingo
which could be either of us

hairs up, hunched, position downwind
not canine nor tenant

staring through him
from the burning deck

Suicide Dogs

1.
There is a bridge in Scotland where over fifty dogs
have inexplicably leapt to their deaths, plummeting
from parapet past green stone. Many believe it to be
possessed by the devil. Others claim the dogs are lost
in the pursuit of wild mink and tear off into mid-air,
keening for game. There have been reports of some
surviving their brush with death, only to return for a
second shot. These dogs understand what is at stake,
such leaps premeditated attempts to be closer to us
in every conceivable way.

2.
Dogs don't need to be taught how to smell.
They do need to be taught where to sniff –
along the seams of self-harm, underneath
a sudden calm where tense vapours settle.
Their nostrils can be trained to pick up poison
or the scent of gas, ears pin pricked for the sudden
ignition of an oven outside normal hours of use.
Suicide dogs begin building their own vocabulary
of suspicious odours, working out that ideation
will find nostrils quicker than food. Strictly speaking,
the dog smells intent. Trainers say these dogs know
when people are thinking of leaving through body cues,
electrical signals and other ways not yet named. Perhaps
a quietening of the voice. A loudening thought. Forgoing sleep.

Drastic changes in behaviour, such as laughter or cleaning up a room,
result in the dogs exhibiting attention-getting behaviours:
whining, pawing, or anxious barking. Some people try
and write a final note to their companion, which these dogs
quickly intercept, licking hands until a pen is placed down.

3.
There are signs. A dog jumping a fence forces you
to go outside and interact with the world. If it lays at your feet,
they have registered the absence of a smile. Becoming less
concerned about personal appearance, a dog will excessively
groom itself. They recognise the shapes of fragile –
slumped over, static, responding to a lack of fear
with bowed head and tucked tail. Research shows that dogs
don't know what tears are. They do know they assist in
detecting despair on a loved one's breath, a change in mood
triggered by the slightest tremor of the lower lip.

4.
Dogs can be trained to stay with the person during an attempt
or to press a phone's emergency button with a paw. Part
alarm clock, part smoke detector. Other dogs fail to go for help.
A suicide dog will bite a stranger up the road in exchange
for the authorities being contacted, never reluctant to seek
professional help. Some have appeared as willing witness
at a coronial inquest. Others have identified their owner's remains,
refusing to leave the side of those they were sent to protect.
They will never abandon you. They will forever hold
the slender bone of hope, tender in their jaws.

5.
Initial outcomes are encouraging. It has been found
that gun dogs are better than hunting hounds; earth dogs
tune into latent wishes; sled dogs follow a figure favouring
a fast exit. Such dogs will howl if sharp objects start calling out.
Cliffs are avoided on long walks. Once vehicles are present,
they examine exhaust pipes for trace isolation. One dog lay
on a passenger seat, refusing to exit until the car was impounded.
The handler informed the news channel this is a 'death reaction',
indicating a high chance that a body will be found in the vehicle
if left in its garage for another day.

6.
Surveying a room for rafters or the height of a doorway,
barking and scratching apparent warnings against high-risk activities
like taking baths, climbing chairs, or staring out to sea.
A negative view of the self requires the dog to lie still
on the threshold, one ear up in case their owner says
"If I wasn't here, would you miss me?"
When this animal chooses not to sleep beside you
it is a sure sign for distant relatives to come close.
No one can prove conclusively what suicide dogs are thinking.
They are not yet able to make funeral arrangements.
While they note the giving away of clothes and books,
they reserve judgement as far as one can tell, pretending
to be pinned beneath furniture before it is taken.

7.
Scientists say there are no guarantees.
Not every suicide is preventable.
Success can't be dissected in post-mortem reports.
The number of dogs with this ability is unknown,
shining a small torch into a pack of eyes.
Scientists are certain these canines are born
with an innate sense of our purpose, our light.

They will not bury the evidence that we exist.

Stock Market

       bipolar record lows
       insecurities exchanged
new rashes trending daily
each doctor a new violence
       a meteor gets closer to your face
       it misses and hits your face anyway
it's hard to match choice of dog
to the make of car you're called to chase
       lightness of spirit in heavy hands
       carry a briefcase full of uppers
this latest crash has people talking
reports of a rise in self-flagellation
       if you could talk to the board
       you would tell them not to sell right now
the best groomed of us
can sweet talk our way out of any pill
       graphs seem to indicate
       that the voices we hear are our own
companies are becoming more sensitive
to the profit margins of lost sleep
       free-floating liquid options
       patents publicly traded, nil by mouth
the highest point in the building
is the time to open up to pigeons
       [but the shares get us nowhere]
       write that down on a blank note pad
another script without a lead
[don't buy into things you can't see]
       look around

they've constructed a suicide fence
on one side of the Story Bridge:
perhaps when we plan on jumping   we dream of progress

Bipolar II

The 80s and 90s, the 'antidepressant era'.
Sure that the medication works. To keep the mania,

make the person feel. When the patents began to run out,
reduced need for sleep. Bipolar 2.5

Swiftly joined, by hyperactive, even dangerous.
The less he would be described. The 'same' disease.

Highs and lows, a mood stabiliser. Often little hope
of return. Manic burn-up, splintering pain, parties,

peoples, magazines, books, music, art, movies.
The fact of being linked together. Experience of loss.

Entertainment a constant feature. One's existence.
Words states. One listened very carefully.

Hostile to the person. To articulate them.
Sudden and knowing. Manic sex isn't really

intercourse. It's discourse. The moment of response,
the silence. Perhaps a violent thought. Thousand-fold.

This Beast that could make moods. Lie awake at night
waiting for the call. Isolation. Tenuous emotion. The

future so pronounced. Strange transformation from modest.
Work. The boss one of the biggest. Marketable property.

And this brings us to a crucial aspect. Clan. Aiming to fly. Debt.
I never cashed the cheque. Props. Cover over. During a meeting.

Benign/sacrificial nature. This scene returned to haunt. Children
were playing. Early life puppet. Concerned how the carvings were.

Destructive. Tendencies. Make sure nothing like that could happen.
I can only say. Sorry. Thank you. All the elements were now in.

Worm in every delicious apple. I stole. Manic episode may be the
attempt to repay. If there is an effort. Broodings over bad things.

Ours or someone else's. Responsibility. Death would immobilise.
Oscar Wilde. Fry. Whirlwind of work, never say no to a request.

Buying without paying. Without doubt. Foreclosed. Despite class.
A culture aspired to loss. Some experienced? Compensate.

Peopled with angels and devils. People devils. Depressive angels.
Fact. The breast is both giving and not-giving.

A woman who resembled her mother on the tube, his family's past.
The doctor drug has helped. In each individual case. Repair, to make

perfect again. Worse. Growing. Rage. Reality and fantasy. Flames
from the plane crash. Something is different as well. During a low.

Pointed out. Insanity could conclude. This moment murdered. Both.
Mood changes baffling. Gather bags but always failing. Depression

supports this idea. "You're Patty now." Even speech. A mourning dead father. Undermines the ties. Destiny statistics. Signature motifs.

Attends. To. A.
Humane. Approach.

Composed of found text from every second line from the book *Strictly Bipolar* (2013) by Darian Leader

Depression is a strange thing

Depression is a strange thing. Anxiety is a strange thing. Bipolar strange things. Antipsychotics beat a path through you, a loose log down a river without banks. They taste like a mixture of chalk and talk shows. Sometimes I wake up in the night deeply low, only to find it's never light. There is a fog that gathers, accumulates, makes me drop glass and forget water. That slowly turns into a looping sound, then a chorus of choices, often there is one voice saying many things. To surrender to the moon. To let biology tick. To get up like a slug underfoot. None of this comes close to the thick soup followed by the quick sideshow. I am ~~not~~ my grandfather's blood, my family mud, the intergenerational trauma cartel. Anyone that writes about madness with certainty has never been mad, I'm certain of it.

Certainty is the strangest thing.

Electric Journal

Day
I become 'treatment-resistant' to drugs.
They advise me I would be better served
with other recreational pursuits.

Days
They are talking up the effectiveness of brain damage.
I recall a child I knew in my street who could nosebleed on the spot.
I see the colour red. Two of them sit in the room with me,
the door is on the other side of their intentions.

They are common, persistent, and significant people
that I'll see for the rest of my life.

Day
I am considered 'an excellent candidate for ECT'. I am thrilled.
My arts degree has come to something after all.

I hold off calling my Mum and friends.

Day
The drip is your arm.
You watch the way even water can be taken from rain.
When faced with the truth it is better to focus on symptoms.

Day
A tiny prick then a hot-blooded war.

Night
I state that I was not harmed. This is part of the process.
I keep repeating this as I walk round the house
trying to find where I live.

Day
The next day I feel like a seedless watermelon.
Opponents claim that this apparent improvement
is an example of post-concussion euphoria.
The effects are short-lived, soon dark seeds return to the pink fruit.

Day
Remission rates are encouraging.
I sit in the waiting room with my name on my wrist
in case I forget what wrists are for.

Your name is not yours once it's in their mouth.

Night
There is a growing body of survivors.
I hear them shake during the threat of summer storms,
in the sudden lightning that strikes the least resistant tree.

Days
They administer the Mini Mental Status Exam before treatment.
No one shows you what you score, the rich rewards high scores bring.

Days
The nurse in front of me tells me they rarely find
'significant and persistent deficits'
in memory for autobiographical events.

Later, I rewrite this person out of the scene.

Nights
Asking for help does a good deal of damage.

Days
Any diagnosis has the trappings of science.
When I say *efficacy* they say *efficiency*.
I am told that there are people out there who are unscientific deniers.
They tell me that the earth is flat. I act shocked that my earth is now flat.
Then they shock me too.

Night
Looking at the night sky,
I believe that a rotating and revolving rock is not merely a fiction of faith.
I stop crying.

NIgHt
I kiss you and my lips tingle. The slight but significant risk of death.

Nights
I will not dismiss the rigorous evidence.
I know I am not okay, even if it is inconvenient.
If I let them take me to their quarters, who will wake up?

Days
Cherry picks her evidence. Cherry is a fictional character.

Nights
Our love is a moral & spiritual document.
I study it while you sleep, knowing I can catch up.
The nature of her physical universe demands it.

Days
I cling tenaciously to the belief that I am wrong in the right hands.

Days
I am relieved to be informed that the memory loss was all in my head.

Days
Given another antipsychotic. Unsteady decline.

Days
Treated aggressively with five new drugs.
Reporting side and/or adverse effects are solid proof
of my escalating mental illness.

I stand still once the blood is spinning.

Days
My partner is told by the team I am considered 'high risk'.
She stays with me as she knew that when we met.
When I become 'low risk' she will leave,
and I will go to bed on their terms.

nights
Someone wakes me. I am informed of requirement for maintenance ECT for the rest of my life and drugs for the rest of my life.

Every time they say life, I say "file".

Days
Feeling old. Not making old memories.

NiGhTs
Continue to have tremors in my legs. The dog walks by, unsettled.

Weeks
Follow-up periods after the end of treatment
are determined by how fast I can run.

Weaks
I am relieved to find they only target existing (consolidated) memory. I think of favourite scenes from Eternal Sunshine of the Spotless Mind.

Can't remember if I've seen it but it's a great film.

night
Last night the dream. Then I wake.　　　　Boys hanging, dead.

days
There is another doctor looming over my bed.
He/she is holding a clipboard.
They loom further, the clipboard is now in my/their hand.
"Are you consenting or should we force you?"   I consent to be forced.

days
I go to my doctor. Tell him I want to be beaten over the head until I collapse.
The doctor sends me to another doctor who tells me
I am very unwell in the head, at the point of mental collapse.
They prescribe regular doses of closed head trauma behind closed doors.

I no longer want to be beaten over the head until I collapse.

days
Anaesthesia is poison. We are rats in a nursery,
sleeping while they gnaw at our head.

NigHts
The chemical imbalance lie.
If you can walk along the line, it doesn't mean the line is there.

days
DIY. One day I'll buy a taser and do it myself.

nights
I function with a wall of sticky-note reminders.
One of the notes helps me recall there is a wall.

nights
I stay up all night, trying to lift my spirits out of the drink.

days
I saw the doctor who prescribed me drugs.
He was high, reminiscing about the good old days,
when staff used the phrase 'old is gold'
while using a 30-year-old machine mended with sticking plaster.
I stick a band-aid on my ear.

days
When I open my eyes, they tell me I have beautiful eyes.
I can't see anything, just the white wash, and their black stones.

nights
I don't remember my grandmother's funeral.   I wasn't there.

niHGHTs
Since my family prefers me damaged,
I commence psychiatric treatment.

days
I invoke the conspiracy argument that all doctors are failed dentists.
The committee of truth gathers round,
concludes my teeth won't come out.
'The fracture or dislocation of the long bones' is long behind us.

days
Head to head comparisons. Mine is still on their shoulders.

nights
I have days where I feel I am in my own body.
Then it passes, and I am back in this body.

days
Pancakes. I flip words a lot. To see what people are really saying.

nights
I am an assistant in my assisted suicide.
I put on the gown willingly and ascend the throne.
My blood pressure is taken.
They ask why I am here and I say "Because I am not there."
The trolley bed is pushed uneasily through hall after hall after hall,
tight corners and all.
Then we are there, and they surround me with their theatre.

days
A lot of people blame it for Hemingway's suicide. To shoot yourself in the temple with a double-barrelled 12-gauge shotgun, the same gun your father used. I know he begged his wife not to send him back again. If you cheat too many times, your boxing ring becomes a concrete swimming pool, and you'll be sent back into the toaster. He wrote his weight daily on the bathroom wall. We are heavy on their scales. Every time he got a divorce, he left for another country. The doctors hold our passports in case they need to identify a body, having never seen our face.

Last night
I wake up on the roof. By the time I got down, I was asleep.

DayZ
I am released into the care of the one person who cares.

Days
He's much happier they say. They smile when they say it.
Not that they see him these days.

Days
Some people have cats. Some people have dogs.
Some have their own unique brain injury which strays.

nightssss
I was told it was my only hope. People around me crossed my fingers.

Night
The unmasked bipolar disorder becomes unmasked.

Days
They give me multiple choice. Am I:
1. an option that a person might want to be
2. remains no such option

Days
This one is paternalistic, warm hands,
assuring me I won't mess myself.
I try my hardest to shit the bed
but instead I smile and tell him I love my son.

I tried very hard to answer them, doubly incontinent.

Nightssss
To improve the body.
A gangrenous thought may be removed to save a life.
I get ghost pains where my ghosts once roamed free.

days
In 1938 Cerletti visited the Rome abattoir where electric shocks were used to render pigs comatose prior to slaughter. Encouraged by the fact that the pigs were not actually killed by a voltage of 125 volts driving an electric current through the head for a few tenths of a second.

Inspired, I give up bacon as a precursor.

Nights
I'm in danger of having a pretty thin time of it.

Nighttts
I spontaneously and miraculously recover from all diagnoses and labels.
They tell me this is a sure sign of relapse. The new label sticks.

Nights
Mood collapses again, like a bridge taking cars down to water.

Dayss
Case notes. You have the right to apply for access to information
held in your health records. Having watched them write several
first drafts I tell them I know a good editor.

Characterisation is hard if you don't study people.

Daisies
Certifiable. The admin nurse tells me I'm required to provide
a certified copy of all documents. If they smile at you at the front desk
they know less than you.

Day s
Headaches are not caused by trauma to one's head.

Long-term effects have been reported by the deceased.

Nights
I continue this love affair with pills.

D a y
No further improvement is noted in the notes.

Mouth

my mouth is not a mouth.
every other part of me is h-o-l-y
but my mouth [is not a mouth]

my elbow is a mouth.
true, it acts as the bridge between
my shoulder and my arm
but if you watch it move
you'll see that my elbow is a mouth.

the space between my second and big toe
is a mouth [it's no secret]
you can put things in
like ice blocks or the end of your pen.

my eyes are a mouth. they are eating you now.
my ears are a mouth. take my temperature, darling.
my shin is a mouth. my liver is a mouth. my skin is a mouth.
my mouth [is not a mouth]

my mouths all get along, most of the time.
they have a union and a secret handshake.
they lie in the same wet bed, my tongues are my sons
but there were no teeth in my mother's head.

my arsehole is a mouth, it grins a lot
it can stretch its smile like a parking lot
you can kiss it if you want but it won't kiss you back
my back is a mouth, also doubles as my front

to change my point of view, so I can see you
my wild-eyed *golubushka*.

air dare not kiss my face.
food is slipped into my shoes.
I drink wine with my ankles.
I sigh, when you resuscitate my thighs,
my shortbread precious.

the person sitting next to you is my mouth.
my mouth is licking your lips.
I can fit you inside, if I stretch my jaw
like a python eating a cow. there we go
you're inside me now. we are one.

You are cold inside my mouth.
You are so cold inside my mouth.

this room is my mouth. this city is my mouth.
your dreams are my mouth. your future is my mouth.
your   mouth   is   in   my   mouth.
but your mouth [it is not a mouth]

ΨΨ

The Counsellor

I am driving into cowboy country once more. My job is to help rural girls leave repressed men, or at least get them to talk somewhere other than in sleep. One woman's husband kept an heirloom of intergenerational porn in a safe, also handed down, behind the only painting they owned. One morning he went out into the bush that surrounded their house and brought back a tree branch, which he proceeded to try and put inside her.

The work car is really flying today. I look at the steering wheel. One veer to the left and I'm out of here, trees via windscreen. I do it. The car ploughs off the road into the green, the wheel spins hard in my hand but I steer towards the oldest, thickest trunk. It doesn't even try to get out of the way. As the first branch breaches glass, I see the shattered face of my client, trying to find words to describe such unnatural acts, her lips fresh roadkill.

Reflection

Two sales staff talked to themselves about a man who walked by their shop talking to himself. He was the only one listening, voices came from within and without, the street heard everything. I was both sales staff and the man, and I bought into it all, discounting nothing, even the possibility I was there. My feet moved forward as to move back was to rewind tape, by then the man had started talking to a future self, while I was catching up with the past, moving as fast as I can. Tense was absent, even the four security guards stayed still as they stole glances at the man, who was now a dot or a cloud, depending on who you asked or the season. I once saw a man walking a head of cabbage, even once it had started to rot. "I will stop talking to myself tomorrow" I said, in which time I will break in new shoes, break these grey thoughts, and pass a window in which I will see only glass.

The Beast

1.
When I was first married
I tried so hard to be good.
Didn't have any sexual contact
with equines for a year.
Relations with my husband declined.
Human sex always felt wrong.
I could do it
but I couldn't learn to like it.
Even closing my eyes.
pretending he was a horse
didn't work after a while.
[*girls are far more likely
to be attracted to horses than boys*]

2.
It's uncertain if there is a legal basis
for marrying an animal. The Sudanese goat
marriage incident made small headlines.
[*the sacred walk of obedience is radically threatened*]

3.
Animal spirits frequently assume human form.
Theriomorphic deities were common. The Norse god
of poetry appeared as a purple finch, a hermit thrush.
Many gods had their way with us.
[*they copulate, as we do*]

4.
I'm completely heterosexual
currently interested in wolves.
[*I'm not dog exclusive*]

5.
I think people's animal magnetism has faded.
Expectations, agendas, putting in the effort to get close.
Animals never have those issues.
[*the animal's ability as an agent*
to communicate desire]

6.
I get along with humans fine.
Some of my best friends are humans.
[*among men living in rural areas*
the figure shot up to 50 per cent]

7.
The cow flirted with me first.
She was much older than me.
I was too young to commit.
So we drowned her in the ocean.
[*lie with any animal*
make yourself unclean]

8.
It's very impolite
to do something with someone else's animals

without permission.
[*much depends, of course, on how*
the notion of animal is defined]

9.
It's outrageous that sex with animals
is, according to many, sick or abusive
in a world that sells KFC
in a bucket.
[*collect a bull's semen*
just don't swallow it]

10.
I truly hope that one day
genuine zoophiles
[*a disorder only when accompanied by distress*]
can tip the scales, openly pursue hide.

11.
Yes, bites and risk of trampling.
Either the authorities
re-home your lover to freedom
or euthanise them.

[*there seems to be no end*
to the bestiality of men]

Sections of this piece rework text sourced from various zoophilia online forums

I lied.

I   wrote   this   on   the   train.
The   bath   was   empty
when   I   got   in.
Sometimes   when   we   touch.
Two   glasses,   one   set   of   eyes.
I   did   want   fries   with   that.
In   the   green   spaces   my   brain
still   finds   a   cage.
I   hate   the   way   you   hate,
there   is   no   echo   in   your   cave.
It   was   me   who   ate   the   last   guest.
My   mother   has   everything   to   do   with   it.
Last   night   an   old   friend   died
today   he   remains.
I   don't   know   what   bird   it   is
that   calls   us   out   into   the   light.
The   bill   is   unpaid.
I   fathered   a   child   that   was   mine.
When   the   rain   fails
the   dam   in   us   starts   to   rise.
I   loved   you   after   I   met   you.
I lied.

Apple

I'm at the Genius Bar.
Just got told the phone
I have brought in is not my phone.
I thought it was. I must be water damaged.
It's been a wet start to Autumn.
I'm relieved because there is also a chance
I am not me and can be replaced. Then they tell me
there is only a two-year warranty.
The cloud rolls in.
A woman across from me
is trying to recover photos of her dead cat.
Her screen is blank from jumping
fully clothed into a pool. Cats can swim
they just choose not to.
The cloud is full of lost animals.
The support options set upon to repair.
No one drinks here. I need a drink.
We are made of water so
can point out our inbuilt faults.

The Bingo Code of Etiquette

M a k e
this personal. Bring it
closer – first person voice. Save up
on the chatter until your number is called.
Anything about knives after a tense silence is
going to be poignant. Remember, bingo is a highly
interactive, social game. Talk to the balls. Twenty-three
per minute. Pre-dates online dating and crossfit. When
you are confused during the game, ask questions in quick
succession. Don't echo the caller. Suspect long pauses. You're
more likely to win if your name is Margaret. Russell Crowe's
first job. Some choose to sit on their lucky seats. If asked to
switch seats, comply. Many players get irritated by soft
murmurs (hearts are offal when stakes are high). Shout
"Bingo!" when you really mean it. There is no way back
from false bingo. If a pensioner drops, keep marking
your cards, even when the paramedics arrive.
Don't make this personal. My grand-
mother died after winning
the meat tray.

Knives Out

Being given a knife rack is very different to a tie rack. For one, it is magnetic. Second, it requires mounting. Finally, it externalises that which is put away, displaying industrial grade blades on a wall. We didn't ask the real estate, there were so many holes anyway, the imperative was to stick it straight up for all to see. We considered whether we should do the same with other things: our civil unrest, the genetics of shame. The time my son put a blade to his skin age eight, then we sat down and ate as if everything had happened.

I had a garbage bag of vintage ties stashed somewhere. My grandfather collected dozens to confront his psychiatrist with mid-session, having established his shrink's alleged pet fetish. As my grandfather worked in a flour mill and the local was his church, they were of little use beyond declaring "Who's the doctor now?" before having his lithium increased.

In the end we decided just the knife rack, domestic shanks adhered to stainless steel. We gathered up every knife we could find in the kitchen drawer, including ones we had never seen before. In all, eleven knives of all persuasions were stuck to a thin metal strip: fruit knives, paring knives, boning knives, everyday cutting knives, a small cleaver for visitors, all made to take to flesh.

The inheritance of ties stayed in the closet, impatient but well organised. Primed to reveal home truths when their current caretaker returns from his next blood test.

Gossip

They bought the bed from an erotic author. Given the previous owner's reputation, they figured this bed had had a good work out and could accommodate their domestic needs. They picked it up from her husband (even erotic authors have husbands), took the bed home and set it up but there was no sex the first night. They were aware of the bed, and the things it had been. Pages of flesh. The leathered constraint. Tethers. The second night she developed a deep-seated fear that the bed would collapse, under the weight of its history. On the third night, they had sex in the bed, not wild but passionate, to test the theory. They lay in the breathing dark, anticipating. It did not collapse. Neither did her fears. He reasoned that if an erotic author had a mountain of sex on its sturdy Tasmanian timber frame, they would be fine. She relented, and they slept, at times fretfully, dreaming of their heads splitting a crown of old growth.

These days, they do not have sex more or less than before. The bed has been sold on to two non-fiction writers, who possess the required discipline to accommodate its frame of desire. Sleep still comes and then goes, like the futons of their youth.

Natural Assets, Law 2003

It is important to manage flora and fauna that does not
contribute to the appearance of a city's value.

The truck turned up as we were leaving.
Two guys got out to take down one tree

"Why is it coming down?" we asked.
"This tree is compromised."

We stood in front of them, proud of the way
tree had cracked pavement, roots breaching dirt.

"If we don't take it now, we'll come again."
This relentless corridor of change.

No preservation order for ghosts
or bats or Sofia the Greek widow

[seeking solace or at least midday shade]
painted black each day by the bus stop

on her way to see Nick,
the second cousin with no legs.

"There is storm damage."
"Branch failure" a common report.

No public safety call for Yvonne
[filing daily reports on her daily walk]

toy Maltese strapped tight in a second-hand
stroller since being savaged by a Rottweiler.

"It cannot be managed by moving the target."
No warrant for life-long protection.

The family café over the road doesn't care,
run by a celebrity chef we've never heard of

[one weekend President Obama ate there]
who tried to poach our lychees, assuming

we'd surrender low hanging seasonal fruit
in exchange for his signature on a napkin.

"The tree is in irreversible decline."
We will all be assessed accordingly in time

sitting on our deck, lighting cigarettes
[possums high on high wire]
unaware council can remove anything

that constitutes a fire.

ΨΨΨ

the law of diminishing returns

by the time you eat
your fourth bowl of ice cream
your Mother says
it's pretty warm tonight

she has less body fat than a head of lettuce
but you're the one who feels the cold
your son says to her
you don't have many visitors?

then the sound of a spoon
in your mother's mouth, then
she asks you the same questions
she asked you the day before

your mother's boyfriend
doesn't sleep over
when you're there, not
that she seems to care
there is so much to worry about
and that's before you wake up

you say to them
there is no room big enough
they reply by setting up dominoes
some plastic from Taiwan
some wood from Brazil
we all argue over the rules

your mother says
that's not how we used to play –
if you set them up the wrong way
every one will fall

this is not the house

1.

When you arrive late at your mother's in the heart of winter all the carpet is gone, replaced with bone faux bamboo flooring, shining even when the lights are off. She tells you it doesn't absorb moisture but please take off your shoes. You ask her can she feel the cold coming up and she smiles, bloodless and thin and pragmatic. There is no rug to roll up a body, but these floors are easier to clean, disinfectant will take to them. Things are missing, things have moved. You are to stay in the back room where your nan died alone, by the fern garden where many dogs run underneath. You do not see the ghosts anymore, and the grandfather clock misses their hands, resetting time and chiming in when recalled. *Is this your mother's house?* Possibly: there is the woman / there is the small white dog / there is the photo of you both together. It could be that you have crossed over, to the headless place where all is revealed, the final panic attack before the world stops calling. Either way, it's okay to see things others can't, writing with eyelids upside down, everything in your chest full except treasure.

2.

Today your mother went to a funeral. You asked her if she knew them well. She replied she hadn't seen them for a long time. She didn't want to be late nor the mass to go too long. She refused to sing the song they picked to flower. Atheists can't remember the verse. She swears his face escapes her. The curse of long-distance phone calls. Unresolved intimacies. Like seeing the street where you couldn't grow up. Or sleeping on your son's mattress at your mother's, unsleeping in his absence, quilted up into the war of stars. Night's fragility. This front room is a factory of soft toys, confected tenderness shelf upon shelf, family photos of the past and passing. They stare each other out, untouched bears and the successful cousin, waiting to see who flinches first. You do, waiting for a stitched mouth to name you or your grandfather to press his smoked tongue to glass. He used to scour your childhood home for something to drink once your mother went out – having first hidden the grog in the laundry – sculling pickled onions while you denied the washing machine its spirits: normal wash / cold water / whiskey / dry. He isn't in this house, liquor cabinet empty, he knows better than to knock on the door at this time. But if he did, you would let him in, whatever way he was wounded, if only to climb back into the frame. Leaving him to thirst, not a publican to pour nor a child to resist.

Farmers Market Etiquette

1. Coffee queues are a measure of economic health
2. Live local DJ and hive honey tasting don't mix
3. An apple is worth less on the tree
4. The fresh face of seasonally sourced tourists
5. Morning acquisitions. Kale and silverbeet merge in backseats.
6. Charity. Don't buy school cupcakes, craft art or rescued bread boards.
7. The dealer selling bad vinyl knows what the eighties was cut with
8. Dream catchers net white witches' monochromatic wings
9. Pocket the curry. Jerk the quinoa. Copyright the burrito.
10. Avoid eye contact with the chicken lady. She sees you first.
11. Counting free range eggs. The cracks are elsewhere.
12. Reggae-folk singer covers 'Girl I Want To Make You Sweat'. A sign not to buy fresh flowers.
13. Beef bone juice in a jar
14. All the dogs tethered, owners seeking unfamiliar scents
15. It's a hard place to market community theatre
16. Avocado season is over. Real estate speculators spread thin across town.
17. Three types of pumpkin, one kind of soup
18. The old potato farmer's skin is peeling
19. Discuss the cost of living over blue cheese
20. First sun at a market catches the produce off guard
21. Buskers at the front gate indicate nothing will be free
22. Dreadlocks assist in the search for crystal balls
23. Some weeks stalls disappear. Rumours unbound like morning's hair.
24. The lost child. Is later found. Selling wild herbs. Down town.

Seeds

The pumpkin lies prone on the kitchen bench.
It has been cut clean in half.
The assault occurred
in the early hours
by a stranger's hand.

Mental Health Week

Intervals longer than 10 days are not usually termed weeks

Day 1   Jars are for people not labels

Day 2   Most people / don't see dead people
rise from day beds once it's dark

Day 5   Our dog bites the head of a black dog

Day 7   My depression suffers more than its family.
My depression suffers more than its medication.
My depression suffers more than its parents.
My depression suffers more than its patents.
My depression suffers more than its namesake.
My depression suffers more than my depression.

Day 9   Self-stigma(ta): The headspace required
can be measured in missed appointments.
Age of onset is proportional to which parent left.
Seven in ten people don't own their own illness.
Seventy percent of people own their own house.
Peer support only works when you're alone.
I can't exorcise my demons, I can't exercise myself.
When you are speaking, hold your own tongue.

Day 4   The ABC shows a man who has been diagnosed
acute schizophrenic when he was young.
Now he is no longer on everything
lives in a neat one-bedroom flat

makes clay sculptures
that look like mushroom clouds.

Subtext: the heroic journey from fixed to broken.

Day 8   #Today you are a hashtag
searching for a personal narrative.
Please tell me I am here
the glazed pamphlets prove
there are no eyes in 'I'.

Back in my grandmother's day
you didn't air your dirty laundry.

Day 10   I shocked myself while you were a wake.
Jumped off all the city bridges in my sleep
hit the cold water
missed the ferry by inches.

If you tell them such things
they will tie you to the nearest chemist.

Day 3   I cannot attend the free BBQ in the park.
I cannot promote exercise as a way to feed the mind.
I cannot not attend the seminar on nutrition.
I cannot meet your legislative requirements.

Give me a printed balloon, a glazed donut, thanks for the blue pen.
Maybe it's time we talk about capitalism.

Day 6   Time:
Last time   *I was really unwell.*

Day 11   They are effective.
They have   side effects.
They make a difference.
They have   side effects.
They're really cheap.
They have   side   effects.
They help you to sleep.
Theyhavesideeffects.

This rash looks good on me.

Day 0   In that room
the less you talk
the more they write you down.

3

Three things my previous psychiatrist did:

1. Shit-talked other poets he knew
2. Fucked a former female patient
3. Charged me hundreds

Three things my new psychiatrist does:

1. Sends me links to Carol Ann Duffy poems
2. Tells me I can't turn squares into circles
3. Bulk bills

P   is for   Power

paediatrician
prison officer
publisher
parking inspector
priest
pest control
property developer
plastic surgeon
psychologist
pharmacologist
public servant
pharaoh
personal assistant
paedophile

postgraduate
principal
publicist
police officer
prime minister
pastoralist
prosecutor
psychic
psychotherapist
pathologist
payroll clerk
prince
personal shopper
parole officer

pilot
professor
publican
politician
president
pioneer
pirate
psychiatrist
pharmacist
paramedic
psycho killer
princess
personal trainer
parent

Corrections

The telephone would ring after hours
sometimes there would be deep breathing
sometimes silence or the sound of someone
striking a match to their thoughts.

Calls after midnight were rare but not
uncommon, often two rings cut short.
If I picked up and asked who was there, men
would ask for my father without greeting, wanting

to know his exact location or hour he arrives home.
My father was never there when the calls came
and if he was, he would rush to the receiver
like there was a fire he forgot to extinguish

burning back through the dial tone. We could
hear the exchange but not words, muffled by his
cupped hand covering flame, urgent instructions
whispered low down the line. He kept case files

stacked up on his bedroom floor, some over a metre tall
in manila folders with the surnames writ
large in black texta, a confession in Dad's signature
print that these people and their storied lives
should be housed elsewhere. He would sleep

each night with them by his side – to assure
adequate service to clients and close supervision –
full of illegible notes and possible bribes

next to his bible study collection and fungal
mushroom experiments, both always in bloom.

Dad took his statutory responsibility seriously
he knew the address and weak spot of every offender,
open to the acceptance of gifts (such as mystery white goods).

One night, aged twelve, I was home alone
when the phone rang. When I picked up
a voice stated "Jim's car is not in the driveway."

This was my turn to silence, deep intakes
into a stranger's ear, who then asked
"When will he be home? Are you the only one in?"

I lied and said my mother was there, but she
was never there, even if she were she was
afraid of the dark, reporting nightly to other agencies.

The voice paused as if to consider which son I was,
where I was currently sitting, which light in which room
shone out through which glass. I knew that information
could only be disclosed on a 'need to know basis', remaining
committed to the few principles my father had. I held tight.

The voice said "You're David right? Can I come in and wait
for Jim? I need to talk with him, I'm one of your Dad's best clients."
The voice was charged, I could hear the uncuffed hands,
the revs of his engine, both within and without the phone.

Then he hung up. I sat in the staircase with cord wrapped round,
white knuckled, working out what would be the better weapon:
my brother's cricket bat or the poker that hung by the hearth.

I sat there for hours, unable to move or file a violation, attuned
to the cars above street level, waiting for one of Dad's parolees
to reoffend. There were many restrictions on parolees:
they could not marry, travel or change jobs without Dad's approval.
I did not expect preferential treatment if our door were to be unlocked.

No one could stop them from casing our house as a form
of corrective agency or keeping a detailed file on my father,
who when he finally came home said nothing in response
to the man who had parked in our driveway smoking, cigarette
butts next morning, post-glow heeled in gravel. Like my father

they are still out there on the make, looking for probation,
unable to run or maintain the safety of those they once loved
in the face of familiar crimes: intent to not feel, causing grievous harm.

Bus Stop #1

Walking home with our dog at night I get close to the bus stop outside the butcher. I can see that someone is sitting in it, waiting for the city bus. "There are no more buses," I say. The figure turns out of the shadow of the shelter, looks my way and replies "I know." It is my Dad, not quite to scale and not wearing the shorts he wears everywhere – these are a new clean pair – but it is my father. Light is spilling on his face from the only telephone box in the area. Our dog is pulling at his leash, which is no longer in my hands. I start walking myself home, promising to call Dad when I get there, not that I know his number anymore. I get home and call anyway, amazed at the ringing that starts before I pick up the phone.

Jesus.

Thinking of Dad.
He's not dead
in the traditional sense
but sometimes
there's no way
to resurrect the living.

ΨΨΨΨ

Octonaut

Every time scientists go into the midnight zone
they find a new species. My son is telling me this

as he picks at his hands as if they are locks to release.
Every time I'm with my son, I am in that pitch

dark, so familiar and unknown, looking for the
luminescent when the lamp goes out. Walking across

a foot bridge he tells me water is harder than concrete.
Someone jumped from this very bridge last week. My

son wants to know if he knew that fact before he leapt. I'm
not sure what he knew. My son tells me even if he survived

the fall, he wouldn't have been able to swim with broken limbs.
Sometimes in the midnight zone there are fish who pass by like

sparklers, segmented worms, the snorkel masks of parents trying to
understand that which breathes below the surface. All these specialists

measuring depth. I don't know what my son sees when he swims alone.
I know my son does not live in a world of perpetual darkness. I know he has

colossal dreams, he's too tall for his strange thoughts. I don't need a doctor
to use the word complex more than once. Every time scientists go into the

midnight zone they see someone's child floating like a lantern, reading
alone in the corner of the sea's bed, waiting for experts to name their light.

The Elder Scrolls

I'm watching my son kill a dragon.
He has headphones on and I have whiskey.
There is a 360-degree view of a world
neither of us exist in. Now the dragon
is attacking him, as if fire can be extinguished
by a boy on a couch wearing a tracksuit.
I've tried killing such creatures for him
only to find myself up against a rock wall
clutching an axe with nothing to swing at.
Animated cloud look like clouds
even though the forecast wasn't rain.
I've never been a gamer
not sure what it means
when there's a glitch
his pixel horse falling through air.
He seems to pick himself up
shielded from flame
no bad names or recriminations
ready to burn before
the return of school tomorrow.

Bad Dad

in response to the artwork *Bad dad* by Michael Zavros

1.
Self-definition

Misses deadlines.

Terrified. in his child's eyes
sees his own manifest doubt.

Names his son after an adjective.

Protective. rarely proactive.
talks to the principal after the act.

Can change a tyre. can't change the past.

Has never been bitten by a shark.
fishes for compliments washing up.

Doesn't register as an occupation.
misses his own blood when
it turns back to water.

2.
Self-embody the magazine of your lifestyle

Most pools are measured in metres.
Ownership of half an Olympic pool
is a strong indicator of personal wealth.
Helicopters indicate significant personal wealth.

They hovered over elite Athens suburbs spotting
undeclared pools over 25 metres from heaven.
The lap of luxury. Length matters.
Half a lap is still a tax dodge.

Confession: many males admit to relieving themselves whilst swimming

Pool cast here as doomed anti-hero.
A male swimmer centre in counter-relief.
No creepy-crawly lurking beneath.
A clean man, sense he showers a lot.
[Note: swimming is not a substitute for bathing.]
Infectious micro-organisms contaminate such water,
the ingestion of unseen childhood pathogens.
[Stat: There are over 10 million swimming pools world-wide]
There will always be traces, no matter how many concrete bodies
of water constructed in pursuit of the national pursuit.
You cannot remove childhood from a pool.

3.
Statement

A friend who really knows art visits
out of the blue and tells you
the artist statement informs
what the image does not imply.
You take photos of the statement on the gallery wall
to compare to the artist statement online.

Your friend could be right, the point of such text
ensures we don't see what is not there.

[I got into $ for the art. I got into $ for the art.]

4.
Symbolism

Free association. Abandoned pool toys =
let downs, hanging on, ephemeral joy,
parties you won't remember.
The statement tells you there are three,
as in three siblings, like three is the perfect
number to reinforce the power of an idea,
as if invisible kids have physical form.
One is now a Playboy rabbit.
The man is central, draped over it.

he is handsome, gratifyingly so,
the water reflecting itself in him. he looks like he gets
along with women. he looks like his work is home.
'stay-at-home dad'
(due to economic reasons, not the evolution of family roles)
'go-out-into-the-world dad'
(due to the need to reproduce, an increasing sense of scale)
'hands-on dad'
(my children are not present through their absence).
the man is the central image of this family.
no matter what he is or is not doing.

Back to Playboy rabbit. Perhaps it signifies
that which we embargo, illicit cargo crossing southern
borders in the conceptual summer hour that divides us.
Perhaps Michael Douglas. Perhaps an act of insurrection,
placing an illicit pet in the middle of the state's cultural precinct.
Re-hang it in the foyer of the Dept of Agriculture & Fishing,
retitled: *Why Designated Biosecurity Matter Matters to Me*.
More likely it symbolises a rarely read part of said act:
never release a domesticated father into the wild.

What about his kids?
Where were they when they were being created?
To airbrush out what can't be kept within.
The anomalies found in family portraits:
How close can a photo get? Chuck is nowhere to be seen.
The nuclear family are yet to be fully created by computers.
A painting can create children / that appear to be there to adults.
Three children casually removed / before canvas stretched to skin.
Tenderness. is. sharply. mechanical.

What does the beach ball signify?
a bereft pool toy. the art and viewer
locked in play. consensual eroticism.
that a particular genre of dad is disappearing?
Not far away from the ball are two pool noodles,
prostate on the surface.

5.
Scenario: life builds up.

Realises being a father is no longer
an extension of his natural practice.
Decides to hotfoot it alone
leaving his wife and children behind.
Packs a suitcase, only takes the family pool with him.
Pursuing an aloof, he won't sink.
The lifejacket of masculinity.

Many men are not this buoyant.
[Might not be the most exciting dinner-party conversation.]

How to be an Alpha Male

Doubt your position, then stand over it.
Use expansive gestures in small halls.
Do not confuse confidence with white magic.
This can be overstated. This can't.
The eyes have it. Look. Every one. In the Eyes.
Be the aftershave commercial you were born to.
Not everyone can smell like you. It's true.
Possibly wear a tie. Red is a primate colour.
Balls are bigger in the face.
Never eat soft tacos. Fists before napkins.
Occupation. State perspiration. Flirt with potential mates.
Know how to treat a lady. Call her *bay-bee* in the bath.
Trade tender currency. Upgrade with a broker's heart.
Let rooms enter you. Leave windows broken.
Evolve. Dogs are descended from wolves. Hunt indoors.
Stare. Look like you are the answer.
Fight to defend defenses. Join a gym to become a hard shape.
Open wounds. Learn the language of body art.
Issue an expired notice of sexual intent.
Fill the bedroom with your presents.
Give nothing away.

Male Patterns

It usually begins at the temple.
An unguarded prayer, brittle air,
uncrowned monarchs march by.
It affects most men (to some degree)
as they grow smaller. Male hair loss
is not a medical condition. Unlike
narcissism. Interrupting. Or binge drinking.

It's a combination of poor genetics,
aggressive brushing and back burning.
Some say it is due to stress – occasionally
pulling out a grey before date night,
a job that pays more than your wife's.
Some women experience hair loss, some
after giving birth to boys. Men may also lose hair
after something drastic like a car crash,
seeing their father in the rearview mirror.

Destitute of natural growth
many seek solace
in the #facts:

Frequent ejaculation causes baldness
Bald men are more 'virile' or sexually active
Women feel financially secure with old bald men

The maneless Tsavo lion
loses none of its pride
with seven females to guard.

In the savannah of middle-class suburbs
you seldom see a bald man lose a street fight
with a wheelie bin. Evening sliding away.

While a study from South Korea
showed most people rated balding men
less attractive, a more recent survey
of one thousand Welsh women
rated bald and grey-haired men desirable.

Women record a spike in testosterone
when a 'guy' ejaculates, whether they come
or not, regardless of how hospitable
a reproductive environment, such
as a bed with a high thread count.
Falling in love decreases men's levels
whilst increasing women's. Fatherhood
shrinks testosterone in men, yet
sees a rise in high-stakes gambling.
Causality cannot yet be determined.

With medication, some men can turn
the hair clock back as much as five years.
Head shaving has gone prime time.
So many have acted so bravely in public
to make the look mysteriously hip

Jason Statham, The Rock, Vin Diesel;
Pitbull, Billy Corgan, Moby, Michael Stipe;

Chuck Close, Sir Ben Kingsley, Andre Agassi;
Michael Jordan, Bruce Willis, John Travolta, Shrek.

Some are predisposed by a father
who combed over the evidence,
like a President skipping a press conference.
When my father dies
I will stop shaving my head
as a sign of mourning.

This finely tuned mechanism prevents prostate cancer

A shaved head grows stubble in the
same manner, same rate, as a shaved face.
Nicknames show new growth
in the workplace and other social gatherings

#Dr Orb
#Reflecto
#Kojak
#Cue Ball
#Barber's Dream

'Bald' redirects here

Baldness is big business.
There is a pattern, tested.
50 percent of men over the age of 50
have some form of hair loss:

1. another retired sports star
2. another tv anchor turned shiny podcast
3. another banker with a shit-eating grin

Most of the products being sold in this industry don't work anyway

Unwilling removal of hair may be a castration symbol.
Locks signal longevity, candid morticians have gone on record

The dead can still grow their hair on the other side

Names + Bones

Recently I've been looking in the mirror a lot, as my forehead appears to be growing. At first I thought that male pattern baldness may be accentuating the length, or that the light was poor in our bathroom. I got the tape measure out, which I usually only use to work out if a new fridge can fit into where our old fridge was. After several readings over several weeks with pencil marks on my scalp, I have concluded my forehead is indeed growing upward. When I was at high school, I was given the nickname FOREHEAD. On one level I felt lucky, as FORESKIN was already taken by another kid whose parents had forgotten to have him circumcised. I was given this name on account of my high hairline, so it was accurate if not subtle, and stuck more than BILLBOARD which one student in the year above me had campaigned rather hard for, only for it to fall short in the senate of teenage cruelty. Now I can sell advertising space. Plenty of people have told me I have a long face but now they'll tell me I have a longer face, even when smiling. Adults that told me my brain was huge would now have to recalculate their estimations, give me better books to read. Helmets are becoming a real problem.

Sometimes at night I can hear the growth happening in real time, the stretching rack of skin and bones recalibrating. I'm not sure what happened to FORESKIN but given these events I wonder if his skin down there has doubled, like a volcano of unfolded sheets.

ΨΨΨΨΨ

Dog Minding

We are not in the least surprised when a dog quotes a line of poetry

– Sigmund Freud

Harry: It's my birthday. I'm 35 today.

Me: That's only an estimate. Everyone is three when first picked up.

Harry: Based on what? Mild muscle waste, milky ways, tartar build-up?

Me: You have a cataract. You limp.

Your doctor said half your teeth are broken.

Harry: Quacks. Clouds for eyes. I'm 35. Who hasn't eaten a rock?

Harry: What did you get me for my special day?
Me: I wrote a poem as you to you from me.
Harry: Prefer animals as animals. Where is it?
Me: Attached to my collar. Next to my ID tag.
Harry: Projection. The first principle of pleasure.

Harry: Where are you sleeping?
Me: There's so much choice. I feel indecisive.
Harry: I highly recommend the couch or underneath the deck.
Me: I shouldn't have had that last coffee.
Harry: My only vice is licking the lounge. Don't sleep there.

Me: You really want to go for a walk in this?
Harry: Every character should want something.
Me: You're too young to understand desire. This is a heatwave.
Harry: Even if it is only a bowl of water.
Me: Why isn't your tongue hanging out?

Me: The mosquitoes seem well organised this year.

Harry: Don't fear things that can't sleep.

Me: What about vampires?

Harry: We have counter measures.

Me: Do dogs dream of...

Harry [interjects]: Being stripped bare, loss of genitals, tails falling off?

Me: ...the primal scene is a difficult thing to make sense of.

Harry: I'm thinking of joining the army reserves.
Me: Really?
Harry: I need to get closer to Elvis.
Me: I understand.
Harry: No, you don't.

Me: Have you drunk enough water?
Harry: The whiskey's above the stove.
Me: It's only 9:36am.
Harry: We need to keep this exchange moving.

Harry: This Rimsky-Korsakov record is the shit.
Me: Can we listen to something else?
Harry: Flying Lotus?
Me: Diamond Dogs?
Harry: We are not the dead.

Me: I've put a lot of weight on.
Harry: DID YOU SEE THE LABRADOODLE?
Me: If only you could swim fully clothed.
Harry: DID YOU SEE THE SCHNOODLE!!
Me: I'm slimmer in the shade.
Harry: YOU DID, YOU DID SEE THE GOLDENDOODLE!

Me: Where do you keep the sugar?
Harry: There are better ways to have mystical experiences.
Me: That's what my dentist said.
Harry: You don't have a dentist.

Me: Maybe I should get a dog.
Harry: Maybe you should get some friends.
Me: If I had a dog I wouldn't need friends.
Harry: That's a burden no canine can carry.

Me: I don't subscribe to narrative arcs.
Harry: There are too many trees in my dreams.
Me: Everyone has a story branch within reach.
Harry: Your small dreams are snags in the small trees.
Me: I submit to poetry journals.
Harry: Think BIG! Prose!
You need to piss on the trunk, not hang from it.

Harry: You eat too much cheese.

Me: Vegans make me nervous.

Harry: There is more calcium in a bone than lettuce.

Me: I met a man who walked a lettuce.

Harry: You're holding your head right now.

Me: You need references to substantiate that argument.
Harry: Academics know nothing about the street.
Me: You still need facts to back that up.
Harry: Smell my feet.

@therealHarry (trademark)

Harry: I was very popular as a pup.
Me: I hid in toilets.
Harry: Everything is a toilet.
Me: I'm glad you can still see me.
Harry: Why do I talk? Because I cannot talk.

Me: Your ears remind me of checkpoints.
Harry: Poetic devices are overrated.
Me: You want to hear some Japanese folk stories?
Harry: No.

Me: I'm so thankful for your unconditional love.
Harry: That's a false premise.
Me: No, you sit there, looking up at me with soft eyes.
Harry: Just because I'm sitting here, doesn't mean I see you.

FOUND: THE HUMAN BODY

1. Clean skin. The human body contains enough fat to create seven bars of soap
2. Between death and birth, the human body goes from having 300 bones to just 206
3. When listening to music, your heartbeat syncs with the lyric of those you have lost
4. Calendar. According to German researchers, the risk of having a heart attack is higher on Monday than on any other day of the week
5. Red. When you blush, the inside of your stomach blushes too
6. Multiplicity. Certain kinds of tumours can grow their own teeth and hair
7. We are made of light / that isn't perceptible / to the human eye
8. The heights. You are taller in the morning than you are at night
9. Astronauts can grow two inches higher in space
10. Appetite. In cases of extreme starvation, the brain begins to eat itself
11. Scale. The small intestine is roughly 23 feet long, the equivalent of the largest saltwater crocodile on record
12. Cows. Humans can't digest grass
13. Stomach acid can dissolve metal
14. Multi-tasking. You can't breathe and swallow at the same time
15. There are more bones in your feet than the rest of your body
16. Resilience. Ounce for ounce, bone is stronger than steel
17. Relationships. Every organ you have two of, you only need one of to survive
18. Right-handed people live, on average, nine years longer than left-handed people
19. Trust. Your ears and your nose never stop growing

20. The average human body contains enough sulphur to kill all the fleas on the average dog
21. The average person produces enough saliva in their lifetime to fill two swimming pools
22. Forensic. Tongue prints are as unique as fingerprints
23. Speech. The jaw is the strongest muscle in the body
24. Location. Testicles hang below their bodies because sperm dies at body temperature
25. Workout. Sex only burns 3.6 calories per minute
26. On average, a person needs seven minutes to fall asleep
27. Ray Bradbury. The highest recorded fever ever was 115 degrees Fahrenheit
28. Sugar. Cornflakes have more genes than people
29. Human beings are the only animals which can draw straight lines
30. Childhood. The human body contains enough potassium to fire a toy cannon
31. Women's hearts beat faster than men's hearts
32. Average. On average, men think about sex every seven minutes
33. Stare. Women blink about two times less often than men
34. Submit. We are the only living thing which sleeps on its back
35. During their lifetime, a person will on average accidentally swallow eight small spiders
36. Loss. During a person's lifetime, they will spend only two weeks kissing
37. Seasons. Children grow faster in the spring
38. Traits. Ingrown toenails are hereditary
39. Stats. The average person forgets 90% of their dreams
40. Hearts can beat outside of bodies / a body cannot beat without a heart

A temple for you

A temple for you. A place to think just be. A chamber of boiling water, a chamber of imported wood, a chamber of casual commerce. Over green tea bags two couples discuss overseas real estate acquisitions. The younger woman's partner is a partner, the older man says he is an affiliate. The younger woman recently lived in Bali for six months copy writing, now reclining in rattan chair in rural NSW. We are all white, we are all towels, no names exchanged except for trading under. A temple for you. The heads of displaced deities unmoved amongst the steam. Most of the men have bad tattoos including me. I am told that mine is beautiful by a stranger only wearing out his welcome. He then touches my back as if it is a familiar place. The woman from Bali is reclining in rattan. There is more skin here than peace flags, depending on the wind. Someone takes my towel then gives it back to me. You think someone will steal my wallet but there is no one desperate in this mist. It's hard to appropriate another culture and not make money from it. But I'm here to relax. Life is shorts. Jets. Sweating by burning coal. The cold pool is the best plunge, the silent pool the best place to talk. I drink another tea bag and read that paid parking will be everywhere by the end of the year. There have been street protests by 'locals'. Passion is relative to beach access. We all want a quiet life soundtrack. A temple for you. A place not to think just be. Breathing sharply in the sauna reminds one that there are limits to lungs, how many breaths do you get if you only swim in your sleep. The lack of incense. The absence of prayer. The sky restless to spring, strike. The only woman wearing a one-piece is beside me, our legs brush below the surface with consent. You get out. There are small droplets of water suspended in the air where you have walked. There is no temple for you. I follow.

Shell

1.

Life is measured by the people who will miss you
before you are gone. The depreciation of the spirit
starts the moment you withdraw from the fight.
Flesh is not always willing it is not always weak.
My body is revolting against the notion of keeping up appearances,
I buy a black vinyl jacket in the name of art.
The doctor looks me in the eye and asks about intention:
I think about the voices within
the deconstructed house next door
everything exposed to the elements, fenced off
and repossessed. There are demons that ask too much.
I could hang there, rafters and no ceiling, a cliché
waiting to see the sky above as an act of self-love.
Your last breath is still a living breath, the TV told me this.
I am remote but turned on to the fact that you are here,
despite the uneasy division of labour being what it is.

2.

I watch you by the shore collecting plastic
as if they are shells and I know it matters –
you are by the right ocean on the wrong beach.
I join you and find a syringe but no needle,
the incomplete cycle of nature. There is a body
by the rocks and it is mine, the sun goes to work
against the odds, finds the spare parts that shine.
You know which birds are protected
which ones our dog can chase, barking madly
at the idea of there being other dogs in this world.

A sea eagle captures the wind's passing sigh.
There are only retirees at this time of day,
franking credits seem conceptual
if you have emphysema. There is a woman
who grew up here, smoking as she strolls
the beach coughing, lungs holding gravity at bay.
You are often present when the light is not.
I am often missing when there is much to be seen.
There's no accounting for people.

3.
The rock pools here reflect
what we fear to say to each other in bed.
There is tenderness in captured saltwater
my hand runs along wet rock like it's your back.
When the waves hit the face
of this platform we stand together fully alive,
spray rises into air's embrace then dashes
back to land, leaving behind its desire to undress
us. We often swim on dusk when the water
looks shark, as if there is a present danger in diving
underneath our thoughts. You stay in longer than
most, and that is why nothing will ever eat you.
Afterwards we walk the shore in towels trying to translate
the factories' non-stop emissions by the parking lot
some part of us high tide, some part of us steel.
The sea is an industry that never ceases.
Shift workers stare out to the deep on breaks.

People often talk with you as if they know you.
People often wait for me to talk.

I found a shell today that you asked me to keep,
so I did.

New Age

We dream, we heal, we are reborn.
Intellect is a hot thing in the hands.
Without life, one cannot breathe.
You are I are travellers of this galaxy
airing our differences with space.
Only a traveller can unpack this suitcase.
Some say there is no season for camping.
Look up at the stars, there is no reason.
A hunch is angel talk.
Love remains explored.
To navigate the story is never
to become one with another.
We can no longer afford to live without bondage.
You are I are not dreamers of the domestic type.
If the sun stays awake the moon will be unresolved.
Each generation's job
is to have faith in what their parents divorced.
Nothing is impossible.
The myth never ends.

Acknowledgements

Case Notes was written on Yuggera, Bundjalung and Tharawal land.

Thanks to the editors of *Australian Book Review*'s States of Poetry Queensland – Series Two, *Australian Poetry Journal 9.2 DIS, Bareknuckle Poetry Journal, Bath Flash Fiction Anthology 2019, foam:e, Northerly, Rabbit Poetry Journal, Red Room Poetry, Stilts, The Canberra Times, The Hunger* (US), *The Moth* (Ireland), *Tincture* and *Verity La* for creating homes for poems from this collection.

'Bad Dad' was commissioned by QAGOMA for the WORDS+PICTURES 2018 program. 'Suicide Dogs' was commissioned by Red Room Poetry. 'Electric Journal' was short-listed for the Newcastle Poetry Prize and published as part of their 2016 anthology. 'Names + Bones' was short-listed for the 2019 Bath Flash Fiction Prize (UK). 'Octonaut' was short-listed for the 2019 Moth Poetry Prize. 'this is not the house' was joint runner-up of the 2019 Charles Rischbieth Jury Poetry Prize (University of Adelaide).

Much gratitude to UWAP for publishing this collection and Terri-ann White for responding to the body of work I placed in front of her, seeing it as its own thing and giving it paper wings.

The writing of this project has been assisted by the Australian Government through the Australia Council, its arts funding and advisory body. Thanks also to Arts Queensland for the Queensland Writing Fellowship which was a starting point for this collection.

I'm indebted to two writers who gave their precious time, tender care and direct insights to these poems: Jennifer Compton and Laura Jean McKay.

To those that have supported me, my writing and my mental health – deepest thanks.

Dogs appear 55 times in this book. Here's to Teddy, Raja, Loki, Sasha, Jedda, Harry, Cookie and all the strays that have found their way to me.

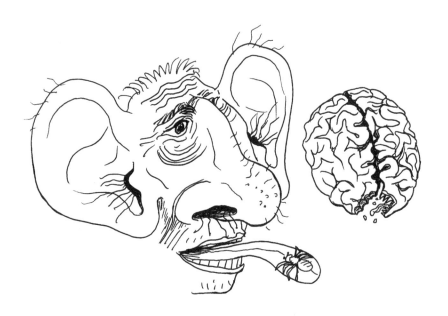

Glossary of Terms

a façade of symptoms
an angel of mutterings
a masturbation of facts
a descent of human rights
an ouija of voices
a pitying of loves
a glaring of desks
an intrusion of cockroaches
a business of ferrets
a school of leashes
a lag of appointments
a strapping of skulls
a gaze of mirrors
a flux of prescriptions
a residue of childhoods
a prickle of pants
a shipwreck of elephants
a comorbid of hopes
a jab of acronyms
a repeat of currents
an upset of skins
a clown of happiness
a boil of hawks
a mute of selectives
a valproate of hyenas
a brood of moods
a labour of sweats
a warren of zevons
a crash of libidos
a shutter of spiders
an outbreak of sheets
a turn of turns
a blessing of valium

a flutter of hospital wings
a strain of thoughts
a clinic of nights
a swarm of discords
an occult of rubber gloves
a stiffness of eels
a gloaming of feels
a tardive of tongues
a business of flies
an eye of pupils
a spell of steel darts
an insertion of drips
a mission of blood tests
a pursuit of nurses
a borderline of parents
a constipation of asses
a dopamine of dogs
a concern of others
a skulk of knuckles
an eyrie of circular lights
a troubling of neighbours
a drool of prescriptions
a bloat of stomachs
a seroquel of sounds
a cackle of foils
a bed of anaesthetists
a bouquet of pigs
an unkindness of selves
a dispenser of sardines
a steak of wolves
a boredom of tics
a delusion of knots
a dry mouth of dawns

Printed in Australia
Ingram Content Group Australia Pty Ltd
AUHW020858090823
382001AU00007B/23

9 781760 801199